Table of Contents

Chapter 1

What Is Weather?

Weather is the state of the air surrounding Earth at a given time. Is it sunny or cloudy? Hot or cold? Rainy or windy? Those are all examples of weather.

Watch a video here!

Weather changes all the time. Clouds move in and bring rain. Then they leave

and the sun shines down.
Knowing what weather is
coming is useful.

Chapter 2

Making Forecasts

Meteorologists study the weather and how it changes over time. They make **forecasts**. These are guesses about what the weather will do next.

Learn more here!

Scientists use tools to collect **data** about the weather. Weather balloons carry these tools high into the sky.

Meteorologists can most easily forecast weather about three days in advance.

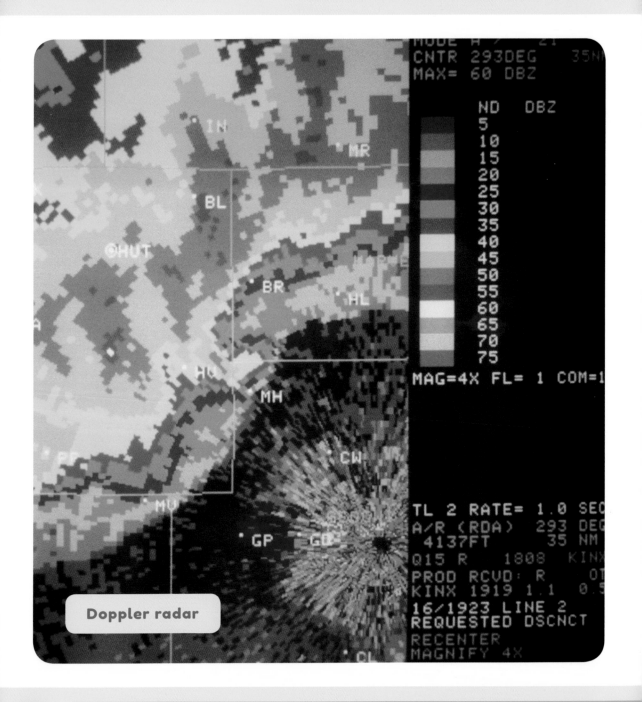

Doppler radar

The tools measure how hot or cold the air is. They record the **humidity** of the air. A **Doppler radar** measures the movement and speed of storms.

Teams of scientists study the weather at more than 100 forecasting offices around the United States.

Chapter 3

Weather Maps

Scientists report the forecast on the news. They make weather maps.

Learn more here!

Weather Map

cold air ⌄⌄⌄   warm air ⌒⌒⌒

Some weather maps show the movement of air. Red lines show warm air that can bring rain or sunny skies. Blue lines show cold air that can bring heavy rain and high wind.

Other weather maps show how hot or cold it is around the country. They show the movement of rain, snow, and other storms.

Chapter 4

Being Prepared

If the forecast is for sun, wear sunglasses. If the forecast is for rain, bring an umbrella. Weather forecasts help people be prepared.

Complete an activity here!

Making Connections

Text-to-Self

Have you ever made guesses about the weather?
What did you see outside that helped you guess?

Text-to-Text

Have you read other books about the weather?
What new information did you learn from
this book?

Text-to-World

Why is it important to be able to forecast
the weather?

Glossary

data – facts or information that is collected.

Doppler radar – a machine that tracks the speed and movement of storms.

forecast – a guess about what the weather will do next.

humidity – the amount of water in the air.

meteorologist – a scientist who studies the weather and makes forecasts.

Index

Online Resources

popbooksonline.com

Thanks for reading this Cody Koala book!

Scan this code* and others like it in this book, or visit the website below to make this book pop!

popbooksonline.com/forecasting-weather

*Scanning QR codes requires a web-enabled smart device with a QR code reader app and a camera.